HOW TO SEND YOUR SNAILS PACKING

... and other gardening conundrums

HOW TO SEND YOUR SNAILS PACKING AND OTHER GARDENING CONUNDRUMS

An exclusive edition for

for all your gift books and gift stationery

This edition first published in Great Britain in 2018 by
Allsorted Ltd, Watford, Herts, UK WD19 4BG

© Susanna Geoghegan Gift Publishing

Author: Becca Law
Cover design: Milestone Creative
Contents design: Double Fish Design Ltd

ISBN: 978-1-911517-54-2

Printed in Croatia

CONTENTS

INTRODUCTION 5

BACK TO BASICS
Starting from scratch 10
Only fools have the wrong tools 10
Transforming tired tools 13
Pointers for the penniless 14
Soil solutions 17
Time-saving tips 18
Tricks with recycled bits 21

SOWING AND GROWING
Safeguarding sprouting success 24
Seedling survival 27
Toughening up tender plants 28
The plant production line 31

GARDENING TECHNIQUES AND MAINTENANCE
Preventing pruning pitfalls 34
Harvesting and storing 37
The art of composting 41
Keeping on top of the rubbish pile 42
The nutrients balancing act 45
Enchanting companion planting 46
Welcome in wildlife 49
Battling bolting 50

KEEPING PLANTS HAPPY
When to water 55
Dealing with drought 56
Fuelling fertility 59
Coping with cold conditions 60
War of the weeds 63
Defeating dreaded diseases 67

GARDEN TYPES

Small places and spaces 73
Dealing with slippery slopes 74
Over Exposure 77
Waterlogged wetlands 78

GARDEN FEATURES AND STRUCTURES

Restoring lifeless lawns 83
Pond predicaments 84
Hedge your bets 87
Supporting spindly stems 88

CREEPY CRAWLY PESTS

Attack of the aphids 93
Ant antics 94
Ghastly grubs 97
The very hungry caterpillar 98
Banishing biting beasts 101
Stingers and suckers 102
On the trail of the slug and snail 105

ANIMAL PESTS

Overcoming pigeon pests 108
Managing moggy misadventures 111
Cracking canine calamities 112
Reducing Rabbit ruination 115
Making nice with mice 116
Minimising mole mishaps 119
Fighting foxy fiends 120
Deer, oh dear 123
Squirrel sorrows 124
Notes 126

INTRODUCTION

Let's face it, it's a jungle out there. From ghastly grubs to slugs and dreaded diseases to lifeless lawns, it's no picnic being a gardener – problems are lurking around every corner.

How to send your snails packing takes a whimsical look at the common conundrums faced by the green fingered community and suggests ways to solve them.

Whether a seasoned gardener or just starting out, this handy and humorous guide to a range of gardening problems is a back pocket must-have. It's packed with plenty of useful tips and practical ideas for avoiding potential pitfalls either in the garden or over on the allotment.

So, grab your trowel and your wellies; it's time to take a deep breath and tackle that garden …

BACK TO BASICS

Starting from scratch 9

Only fools have the wrong tools 10

Transforming tired tools 13

Pointers for the penniless 14

Soil solutions 17

Time saving tips 18

Tricks with recycled bits 21

Gardens are not made by singing 'Oh, how beautiful,' and sitting in the shade.

Rudyard Kipling

STARTING FROM SCRATCH

Any new garden or plot can seem overwhelming at first, especially if it is smothered in weeds or riddled with rubbish, but with a bit of time and patience anything is possible.

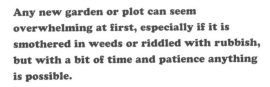

Start by thinking carefully about how you are going to use your garden. For exclusive entertaining? As a play area for the children? For a yoga retreat? All of the above?

Be realistic about the amount of time you have to tend to your precious plot, and the space you have available. For example, artificial grass may be more sensible than laying turf if you have no time to maintain a lawn and no space for a lawnmower!

Create a simple design with measurements and think about the materials and any associated costs you'll need to make it happen. Don't forget the mundane; do you need storage or want somewhere to sit? Take your time at this early planning stage to avoid making costly or time consuming changes later.

ONLY FOOLS HAVE THE WRONG TOOLS

Without the right tools, gardening can be a real chore and simple tasks become difficult and time-consuming. Regardless of your experience, there are a few essentials that no gardener should be without.

- A good pair of gloves will not only protect against general dirt, thorns and painful splinters, but also save a fancy manicure.

- A fork is perfect for digging over tightly packed earth before planting, or adding compost or manure.

- A spade is useful for moving large amounts of earth from one position to another or for digging holes for trees and ponds.

- A trowel will help you to tackle those annoyingly tricky areas that are hard to reach with a fork.

- A rake will allow you to level out the soil after digging and even out those lumps and bumps.

- A hoe is a real must. Use it to remove annual weeds, break up soil, prepare for sowing. The list is endless...

- Unless you're planning on lugging armfuls of soil and weeds backwards and forwards, get yourself a wheelbarrow.

- Don't blunt your kitchen scissors. Invest in a pair of sturdy secateurs for all your pruning needs.

- And lastly, don't forget the wellies ...

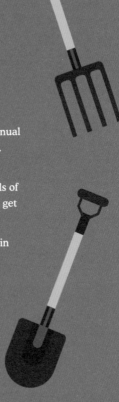

The more help a man has in his garden, the less it belongs to him.

William M. Davies

TRANSFORMING TIRED TOOLS

Keep your tools in tip top condition and they should last you a lifetime.

- Rinse cultivation tools after use to remove soil. Soak any welded on mud in water and then wipe it off with a rag. Once dry, apply some vegetable-based oil with a cloth to help prevent rusting.

- Look after wooden handles by cleaning and sanding off any rough bits and then applying teak oil.

- Store tools away from direct sunlight and out of the wet to ensure they last longer.

- Wipe off any ingrained dirt on secateur blades with wire wool, then give them a rinse in warm soapy water. Dry thoroughly and give the moving parts a spray of lubricant such as WD-40.

- Use a screwdriver to tighten up the screws of any moving parts.

- Keep pruning tools sharp using a file or sharpening blade.

POINTERS FOR THE PENNILESS

Feeling strapped for cash but want to transform your outside space? Sadly, the fabled money tree does not exist, but gardening does not have to break the bank.

- When selecting gardening tools, don't be lured by brand new sparkly spades. A wealth of tool treasures can be unearthed from local online sale sites and car boot sales.

- Where possible, grow from seed rather than buying established plants.

- Investigate local seed swaps on social media or online and marvel as no money changes hands!

- Split plants or take cuttings, then move these to other parts of the garden or swap them.

- Have a go at making your own compost from vegetable peelings, newspaper, grass clippings and other green waste from around the garden.

- Save money on expensive gym memberships and use your garden for exercise. Put your back into it!

- Sow herb seeds to avoid the need to buy expensive herb pots and packets in the supermarket.

Investigate local seed swaps on social media or online and marvel as no money changes hands!

Gardener's Recipe: One part soil, two parts water, and three parts wishful thinking.

Anon

SOIL SOLUTIONS

Unless you've been blessed with luscious loam, it's likely that as some point your soil will need a bit of care and attention. Plants want to grow. If you look after the soil, the plants will look after themselves.

All soils can be improved, regardless of whether you've got gritty and grainy sandy soils that don't retain moisture, or the soil of extremes, clay, which forms a waterlogged mess when wet but bakes to an impermeable desert-like crust in the summer.

Adding organic material is your best bet; digging in compost or manure will not only improve the structure of soils that need it but also increase fertility and water retention.

The pinnacle of soil types, peat, is formed over literally thousands of years in wetlands. This means that reserves cannot be replaced, so always select commercial composts with care and never choose those with peat.

TIME-SAVING TIPS

Life has a tendency to get in the way of getting stuff done and this is no less true for gardening.

It's easy to become disheartened when what started out as a haven for botanicals becomes a weed ravaged and under-pruned mess. Try to be realistic about the time you have available for your garden or plot. Keeping things simple will mean less time for maintenance. Selecting plants that require little care, and avoiding invasive plants, will save a lot of regular pruning and cutting back.

Left unchecked, weeds will overwhelm a garden. Catching them early before they have time to establish will save you from a seemingly endless weeding slog. Applying a mulch of compost or bark will help keep weeds down in the first place, with the added bonus of locking in moisture, meaning less time needed for watering!

Gardening is an outstanding stress reliever, so by repositioning your garden in your mind as a place to exercise and relax you may well find yourself in it more often.

Gardening is cheaper than therapy and you get tomatoes.

Anon

In almost every garden, the land is made better and so is the gardener.

Robert Rodale

TRICKS WITH RECYCLED BITS

- Raise seedlings or simple salad leaves and herbs in plastic recycled pots and packaging. This works best with opaque containers (plant roots generally don't like sunlight). Make some holes in the bottom of the container to aid drainage.

- Create and use paper pots to pot up seedlings. They are quick, simple and free to make and the paper will degrade naturally in the soil once planted. Wrap sheets of newspaper around a rolling pin or can, remove it and then fold the bottom ends of the paper up to create the base.

- Don't throw away egg shells – crush them up and use them around delicate seedlings to deter slugs and snails. Use the empty egg boxes to chit potatoes.

SOWING AND GROWING

Safeguarding sprouting success 24

Seedling survival 27

Toughening up tender plants 28

The plant production line 31

SAFEGUARDING SPROUTING SUCCESS

Getting seeds to germinate can be a bit of an art, and often requires some trial and error.

It sounds obvious, but not all seeds are the same when it comes to germination. Some seeds need nice warm snuggly conditions (a warm window sill or airing cupboard) and others prefer a chillier environment (a frost or a fridge). Some take a few days to germinate and others can take a month. To avoid an epic sowing fail, always read the packet to check the conditions your chosen seeds will prefer.

The amount of water your seeds receive can make a huge difference. Overwatering seeds can cause them to rot, but without enough water, the seed casing will not soften enough to allow the shoots to emerge and germination will fail. Use a water spray to keep the soil damp to touch, but not waterlogged.

If you plant seeds too deeply, your poor seedlings won't have enough reserves to reach the surface and will perish. Generally, a good rule of thumb for sowing is the smaller the seed, the less deep you will need to plant it.

One of the healthiest ways to gamble is with a spade and a package of garden seeds.

Dan Bennett

Seedlings can be very delicate and have diva-like tendencies so always handle with care!

SEEDLING SURVIVAL

Your precious seedlings have germinated. Like small children, they are now totally reliant on you for survival.

One of the most common seedling snags is a lack of light. Without enough of it, seedlings will develop long legged stems, similar to supermodels, as they crane upwards in search of light. To avoid spindly stems, position seeds so they have plenty of natural sunlight or install an LED lamp.

Water plays an important part in seedling survival; crispy leaves are a sure sign of lack of water but overwatering can lead to damping off – a fungal condition where seedlings will simply keel over.

Only think about transplanting seedlings when they have developed at least two 'true' leaves. These are the second set of leaves that develop after the more oval 'seed' leaves. Seedlings can be very delicate and have diva-like tendencies so always handle with care! Only ever lift seedlings by their leaves and support the roots and surrounding soil with a plastic spoon or fork.

TOUGHENING UP TENDER PLANTS

Not unlike stroppy teenagers, young and tender plants can get stressed when they are exposed to conditions they do not like.

This stress is often due to a sudden change in temperature – from warm to cold – and can shock plants so severely that growth is stunted. To avoid such shock tactics, all tender plants will appreciate a bit of time to acclimatise: a process known as hardening off.

Gradually increasing the time that plants spend outside will toughen them up and prepare them for their life in the ground. Plants from the garden centre, seedlings and cuttings should all get this acclimatization treatment.

 As plants begin to harden off, their leaves become thicker and waxier, making them more resistant to changes in temperature. But remember that hardening off does not mean a plant is frost resistant!

I consider every plant hardy until I have killed it myself.

Sir Peter Smithers

There are no gardening mistakes, only experiments.

Janet Kilburn Phillips

THE PLANT PRODUCTION LINE

It's easy to maximise your plant numbers without paying a single penny.

Self-seeding

Many plants will naturally self-seed. Allow seed heads to dry out completely and disperse their valuable bounty before you pull up the old plant. Then just wait until Spring for the new seedlings to germinate.

Collecting seed

Much like a family stuck at home together on a rainy day, splitting plants helps to prevent them from becoming overcrowded and unhappy, with the added bonus of brand new plants! It's easy to split clumps of perennial plants, either by hand or by using a spade.

Taking cuttings

Amazingly, many plants can regenerate from a single piece of stem (or root in some cases). The best time to take stem cuttings is first thing in the morning when a plant contains higher amounts of water. Use a sharp blade to cut the stem just below a leaf bud and then remove the lower set of leaves. Pop the cutting in a pot of compost, water it and cover with a transparent plastic bag. Within a month your cutting should have established roots and be ready for planting out.

GARDENING TECHNIQUES AND MAINTENANCE

Preventing pruning pitfalls 34

Harvesting and storing 37

The art of composting 41

Keeping on top of the rubbish pile 42

The nutrients balancing act 45

Enchanting companion planting 46

Welcome in wildlife 49

Battling bolting 50

PREVENTING PRUNING PITFALLS

Left unchecked, more vigorous plant varieties will develop into an unruly mass of branches and twigs that start to overwhelm and smother other plants in the surrounding area.

Pruning has a number of benefits: it obviously helps to reduce the size of overly large plants but also allows you to remove dead or diseased wood, encourage healthy new growth and perhaps, most excitingly, to clip plants into the shapes of fantastical beasts.

All you need to prune is a pair of secateurs. Keep these clean – to avoid the spread of disease – and sharp – cuts made with a sharp blade will heal more quickly than those made with a blunt blade. Use the secateurs to snip just above a healthy bud (where new growth will appear).

A severe hair cut is not always a bad thing, but beware: pruning at the wrong time, or pruning too much, can severely damage or even kill a plant.

A similar technique to pruning, called 'pinching out', is pretty self explanatory. The tips of plants are literally pinched off to promote bushier growth and prevent plants from getting too long and leggy.

You know you are a hard-core gardener if you deadhead flowers in other people's gardens.

Sue Careless

Nothing ruins an appetite more than gnarled and woody veg.

HARVESTING AND STORING

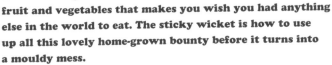

If you've got a veggie plot or an allotment, you'll be familiar with the seasonal glut of fruit and vegetables that makes you wish you had anything else in the world to eat. The sticky wicket is how to use up all this lovely home-grown bounty before it turns into a mouldy mess.

Many a gardener has returned to a plot to find once dainty courgettes transformed into monstrously-sized marrows. Nothing ruins an appetite more than gnarled and woody veg. The vast majority of home-grown produce tastes so much better when still small and tender so grab it while it's young. Not only will your recipes pack more punch but you'll also encourage your plants to produce more.

However you plan to store your crop, be sure to remove any signs of disease or damaged produce beforehand so it doesn't spread and spoil everything else.

HARVESTING AND STORING: TIPS

- Too much for your plate? Freeze it! Fruit, veg and even herbs can be frozen.

- Conquer the tomato glut and make sauces and preserves. Or get pickling!

- Raw root veg like parsnips and carrots can be stored in sand in a cool shed.

- Share it with others! Family, friends, neighbours, your local soup kitchen … The list goes on …

In the Spring, at the end of the day, you should smell like dirt.

Margaret Atwood

Gardening is a matter of your enthusiasm holding up until your back gets used to it.

Anon

THE ART OF COMPOSTING

There is nothing more useless than a compost heap that isn't composting. Keep your heap happy by following a few simple composting rules.

A good compost heap relies on humble anaerobic bacteria to break down organic material slowly over time. Like any living creature, these wee beasties prefer certain conditions.

To survive, anaerobic bacteria need moist conditions with plenty of air circulating. If your heap is too wet, the water will seep into all the air pockets in the heap and you'll end up with a smelly slimy mess. Conversely, not enough water and your heap will be dusty and dry. Both scenarios can be resolved easily: cover your heap with a piece of carpet to keep out the worst of the rain and water your heap if it looks too dry. Turning your heap every now and again will improve air flow and keep those bacteria happy.

When it comes to what to put into your compost heap there are dos and there are don'ts. Vegetable peelings, grass clippings, newspaper and annual weeds all get the seal of approval. Aggressive perennial weeds do not – they will hijack your heap and run riot. Avoid adding raw fish or meat, or cooked food, which will attract foxes and rats; animals most gardeners could do without.

KEEPING ON TOP OF THE RUBBISH PILE

Garden maintenance does have a tendency to create mess. Mountains of weeds, prunings and other miscellaneous debris can quickly pile up like massive mole hills.

Recycle or reuse it

Consider whether any plastic rubbish can be recycled or reused either in the garden or on an allotment. Plastic sacks from compost or gravel have a range of uses from storing, to warming up soil ready for spring plantings.

Put it on the compost heap

Grass clippings, annual weeds and leafy prunings
can all be hurled onto the heap.

Put it in the recycling bin

Any woody material that is too thick for the compost
heap, or perennial weeds, can go into your garden
waste recycling bin. Your council will compost it at
a high temperature.

Burn or incinerate it

Bonfires and incinerators are a useful way
of getting rid of any annual or invasive
weeds that cannot go on the compost
heap. It's also great for any diseased
material that you want to keep well
away from your healthy plants. Many
inner city locations and allotments ban
bonfires, so double check the rules in
your area before striking that match.

We come from
the earth.
We return to
the earth.
And in between
we garden.

Anon

THE NUTRIENTS BALANCING ACT

Different vegetable crops have different nutrient needs. Some greedy individuals suck vast quantities of valuable nutrients from the soil, whereas others put them back.

Crop rotation (rotating where you plant your vegetable crops each year) helps you to maintain soil fertility across your vegetable plot. The basic idea is to avoid planting the same types of plants in the same spot year after year. Doing so not only prevents an imbalance of nutrients but also a build-up of pests and diseases that favour one particular type of veg.

Heavy feeders like tomatoes and sweetcorn strip the soil of nutrients, whereas veg such as legumes (peas and beans) actually fix nitrogen in the soil, making it more fertile for the next year of planting.

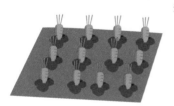

Crop rotation is nothing new. Farmers were using this technique as early as 6000BC to rotate cereals and legumes.

ENCHANTING COMPANION PLANTING

Companion planting is an age old method of planting two different species closely together to benefit one or both of the plants. Companion plants can act as sacrificial foliage by luring pesky pests away, or can simply mask the alluring odour of other vulnerable plants due to their strong scent.

The allium family (onions, leeks and garlic) work wonders at protecting carrots from carrot root fly (who amazingly can detect carrots from up to a mile away!). When planted alongside, the strong smell of the alliums effectively masks the carroty smell, so your tender veg remain undetected.

Try sowing nasturtiums alongside lettuces and beans. Pests such as aphids and caterpillars will happily munch away on the sacrificial nasturtium leaves, leaving other highly prized crops with less damage.

Mint works well to deter moles, as well as rodents such as rats and mice. As an added benefit it also provides a delicious herb for all manner of culinary delights and, when brewed with hot water, a refreshing change to your standard cuppa.

A garden is not a place; it is a passage, a passion. We don't know where we're going; to pass through is enough; to pass through is to remain.

Octavio Paz

We do not see nature with our eyes but with our understandings and our hearts.

William Hazlitt

WELCOME IN WILDLIFE

Many of the most common and stubborn garden pests can be reduced effectively simply by encouraging local wildlife. This natural biological control is free and completely organic.

Invest a little time in creating a small pond for frogs and toads. Toads are active at night, when conditions are cooler and wetter, and will gorge themselves on slugs, helping to keep mollusc populations down.

Consider leaving part of your garden or allotment wild to encourage hedgehogs. A simple pile of leaves or logs in a corner can tempt in prickly friends who will delight in eating up all manner of garden pests, including destructive caterpillars and grubs.

Do your best to encourage birds into the garden by providing feeding stations and by planting cover from predators. Birds such as the song thrush love nothing more than bashing snail shells on a stone plinth to get at the mollusc inside.

Not all bugs are bad for the garden. Learn to recognise ladybirds (and their much uglier larval forms), who will devour aphids that are set on demolishing your precious plants.

49

BATTLING BOLTING

When the conditions are right for leafy veg to reproduce, the plants put all their energy into producing seed. This process, known as bolting, can happen annoyingly quickly. One minute your lettuces are picture perfect globes, ready for harvesting, and the next a monstrous leafy spike has sprouted from the centre.

Crops such as lettuces and spinach are particularly prone to bolting. In hot summer periods it can seem as if your entire salad bed is intent on sending up spikes. The remaining leaves are pretty inedible – the chemical changes in the plant result in distressingly bitter greens, which will see you gurning like a pro.

Bolting is caused by longer periods of daylight, heat and a lack of water in the soil. To reduce bolting, grow your greens in shadier conditions or between other taller plants. Planting varieties that are less susceptible to bolting in the first place will also help.

The chemical changes in the plant result in distressingly bitter greens, which will see you gurning like a pro.

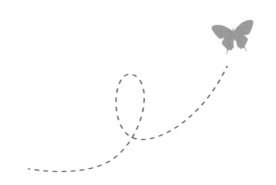

KEEPING PLANTS HAPPY

When to water 55

Dealing with drought 56

Fuelling fertility 59

Coping with cold conditions 60

War of the weeds 63

Defeating dreaded diseases 67

Don't be surprised if you end up having to water your container gardens more than once a day.

WHEN TO WATER

During the long, dry months of summer, the garden should be kept well-watered in order for plants to survive any drought and thrive.

Rather than wait for your precious plants to show visible signs of distress, it is sensible to start watering early to ensure the soil stays moist a good few inches below the surface. If the soil has already dried out to this level, affected plants should be given a prolonged, thorough watering that reaches right down to their roots. To avoid loss of moisture through evaporation, always water either first thing in the morning, before the heat of the sun, or during the evening when the temperature is cooler.

Plants in pots and containers

Don't be surprised if you end up having to water your container gardens more than once a day. Heat, wind and dry air can quickly parch your plants. Terracotta pots, hanging baskets made from coir and metal pots all can dry out ridiculously fast on a hot, windy summer day.

Over the season, you will probably get to know which containers need to be checked more than once a day, but when they are first planted, it's a good idea to check your containers in the morning and again in the afternoon.

DEALING WITH DROUGHT

In dry summers when the sun beats down mercilessly and lawns turn a parched yellow, once lush green foliage can curl and wilt.

Top tips for making your garden more resistant to drought:

- Select drought resistant plants. Those with silver/grey green leaves reflect the rays of the sun, making them much more tolerant of baking hot summers.

- Organic matter retains moisture, so digging in plenty of garden compost or manure into your soil will help prevent your beds from baking to a solid crust. Always water in new plants thoroughly and use a layer of mulch on top to prevent water from evaporating so easily.

- Remove rogue weeds as soon as they appear – they will suck up water that should be going to your thirsty plants!

- Use water retaining granules in hanging baskets and pots. When watered, the granules swell up like tiny water balloons and release moisture into the soil over time as it dries out.

- Install a water butt to collect rainfall runoff from your roof.

Domestic wastewater (known as grey water) containing soaps and detergents is to use for watering. Avoid using water containing bleaches, disinfectants or stronger cleaning products.

Gardening requires lots of water – most of it in the form of perspiration.

Lou Erickson

My rule of green thumb for mulch is to double my initial estimate of bags needed, and add three. Then I'll only be two bags short.

Anon

FUELLING FERTILITY

Want a garden reminiscent of Babylon? Spoil your soil and treat it to a little something extra. Your plants will thank you for it.

When preparing soil, you can't go wrong with commercial composts (as long as you avoid those that feature peat), but this can end up being expensive if you've got a large garden or plot. If you have the time or inclination it's well worth making your own garden compost or leaf mould.

If you're close to a farm or stables, animal manure is a good bet. The stuff stinks – there is no denying it – but it is rich in nutrients. Avoid adding unrotted manure directly to your beds as the acids in the mix will fry your plants.

COPING WITH COLD CONDITIONS

Come Winter, Jack Frost grips our gardens with his icy touch. This sparkling world may be beautiful but without protection, his icy tendrils can leave your plants limp and lacklustre.

As air temperatures dip below zero, the water inside plant cell walls freezes. Unless your fronded fancies are sturdy frost resistant specimens you may end up saying adieu.

Various methods of planning and protection will help ensure your Spring sees healthy plants. Popping tender plants in pots will enable you to move them into the greenhouse or house at the first forecast of frost. For those exposed plants that must endure the cold, protect them with cloches or horticultural fleece. Where possible, leave old plant growth over the winter, rather than pruning it back. This will help to protect the core of the plant during cold snaps.

Frost isn't all bad. It can be beneficial to the gardener, helping to break up the soil for planting in the spring, and providing perfect conditions to stimulate germination of certain seeds and bulbs.

Unless your fronded fancies are sturdy frost resistant specimens you may end up saying 'adieu'.

A weed is a plant that has mastered every survival skill, except for learning how to grow in rows.

Doug Larson

WAR OF THE WEEDS

One of the most common battles any gardener faces is the never-ending war with weeds. Left unchecked, the little blighters can very quickly dominate a plot or garden, overwhelming other plants and starving them of nutrients and light.

The best way of tackling these irksome individuals is to take a little-and-often approach to weeding. This will save you a huge amount of time and effort in the long run. Pull out young 'weedlings' before they can develop into Herculean specimens, which are harder to remove.

Spring is a good time to start getting on top of a weed problem, as the soil starts to heat up and weed seeds begin to germinate. To keep weeding less back-breaking, and to speed it up, invest in a hoe to quickly nip off the tops of annual weeds.

Consider covering any empty patches of earth with plastic or a layer of mulch (such as compost or leaf mould) to keep weed numbers down.

WAR OF THE WEEDS: TIPS

- Annual weeds can simply be pulled up or chopped off at the base with a hoe. Aggressive perennial weeds will need more a more persistent digging approach. Try this first before you reach for the weed killer; sometimes a bit of physical force will do.

- Smother them! All plants need sunlight to survive, including weeds, so cover them up with newspaper, followed by a mulch of compost. If any push through, add another layer of newspaper and mulch on top. Watch with glee as they slowly exhaust their central reserves and give up.

- Use ground cover plants on any bare patches of earth. Not only will these crowd out any weeds trying to make it to the surface, but they also look rather lovely too.

When weeding, the best way to make sure you are removing a weed and not a valuable plant is to pull it out. If it comes out of the ground easily, it is a valuable plant.

Anon

A garden is always a series of losses set against a few triumphs, like life itself.

May Sarton

DEFEATING DREADED DISEASES

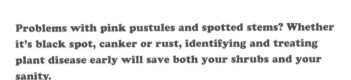

Problems with pink pustules and spotted stems? Whether it's black spot, canker or rust, identifying and treating plant disease early will save both your shrubs and your sanity.

It's always a good idea to be on the lookout for anything unusual that appears on plants: spots, mould or unnaturally curly leaves are not the sign of a healthy plant and should be your first cue that something bad is brewing. Many common plant diseases are easy to spot and therefore treat, but more unusual symptoms will need a more in-depth examination alongside a plant disease guide.

Left unchecked, diseases can spread to other plants so as soon as you spot anything out of the ordinary, a good rule of thumb is to cut out the diseased foliage and burn or hot compost it (the council garden waste recycling bins will do). Unless you want your entire garden to become an incubus of disease, never toss diseased material onto the compost heap.

DEFEATING DREADED DISEASES: TIPS

- Check plants for visible signs of disease before you bring the beauties home from the nursery or garden centre. Avoid anything that looks sickly, regardless of the cut down price.

- Promote good air circulation between plants by allowing plenty of space between them and, if necessary, prune out excess vegetation if conditions become cramped.

- Water first thing in the morning. Many diseases thrive in damp, cool conditions so watering earlier in the day allows your plants to dry off before temperatures dip at night.

If you are not killing plants, you are really not stretching yourself as a gardener.

J. C. Raulston

GARDEN TYPES

Small places and spaces 73

Dealing with slippery slopes 74

Over exposure 77

Waterlogged wetlands 78

Make sure all your plants are multifunctional marvels that really earn their space.

SMALL PLACES AND SPACES

Do you have a petite patio, baby balcony or small-scale front step? Don't despair: all good things come in small packages. Even the tiniest space can be transformed into a horticultural utopia with a bit of imagination.

Start by getting creative with your space. Think carefully about different ways the space can be used.

- Hanging baskets save valuable ground space and can be used to grow strawberries and other fruits and vegetables, as well as standard bedding plants.
- A lack of beds doesn't mean no plants! Pop it in a pot or other container!
- Think tall! A whole host of plants can be trained to grow upwards, either on fences or walls or up cane supports.
- Consider built-in storage options that offer dual functionality, such as a bench or seat.
- Will that statuesque shrub look good in winter? Make sure all your plants are multifunctional marvels that really earn their space.
- Consider splitting up your garden into 'rooms' to maximise the space you have. This will break up the space and make your pint-sized patch seem bigger.

DEALING WITH SLIPPERY SLOPES

Unless you have the grace of a mountain goat, gardens with gradients are notoriously awkward to access and can be prone to drying out. But mountainous terrain doesn't have to mean dull. Sloping gardens can make for incredibly interesting spaces.

- Make good use of gravity! Natural slopes are perfect for water features, including waterfalls and water spouts.

- Plants don't care if earth isn't flat so creating a banked border can make the best use of any hilly terrain. Fill your border with low maintenance plants that won't see you heading for the secateurs every other week.

- Manicured lawns are completely impractical and nigh on impossible to mow in undulating areas, but less formal grasses and wildflowers will be completely content.

- Terracing a slope can give you valuable flat space for lawns or planting.

Fill your border with low maintenance plants that won't see you heading for the secateurs every other week.

There's little risk in becoming overly proud of one's garden because gardening by its very nature is humbling. It has a way of keeping you on your knees.

Joanne R. Barwick

OVER EXPOSURE

Exposed hilly or coastal gardens come with spectacular scenery, but their squally winds can erode soil and flatten your plants.

Protecting plants with wind breaks is a ready-made solution but avoid solid barriers. They have the unfortunate habit of falling flat and can actually increase local wind speeds, making the problem worse.

The most successful exposed gardens feature wind resistant plants which grow in low level tightly bunched clumps, making them more resistant to being buffered by strong winds. They tend to be covered in small, shiny bobbly leaves that do not snag and snap when caught by sudden gusts.

Don't fall into the trap of planting larger, more established specimens in an exposed plot. Without a grounded root system, the wind will literally wrench them from the ground. Younger, smaller plants will develop a good set of roots over time that will anchor the plant into the soil.

SOGGY GARDEN SOLUTIONS

Heavy rain and clay soils can lead to a marshy mess. If water cannot drain away, it fills the air spaces that surround plant roots, preventing them from accessing all the nutrients they need to survive. This can cause the roots to rot and the plant will eventually drown.

To avoid quagmire-like conditions, incorporate gravel and organic matter into the soil to improve the structure and help water to drain more easily. Check all your drains are clear so that water can drain freely. Concrete drives prevent rainwater from draining, making flooding worse, so choose gravel instead.

Never tread on waterlogged soil – it will become more compacted, making your soggy situation so much worse. If you need to access waterlogged ground, create a path with planks of wood to distribute your weight evenly across the soil.

To avoid quagmire-like conditions, incorporate gravel and organic matter into the soil.

GARDEN FEATURES AND STRUCTURES

Restoring lifeless lawns 83

Pond predicaments 84

Hedge your bets 87

Supporting spindly stems 88

Aim to mow little and often; once a week from Spring through to Summer is ideal.

RESTORING LIFELESS LAWNS

Balding, thinning or in need of a good cut? Not time to head to the hairdressers but a reminder to give that lawn a little love.

It's terribly tempting to cut grass short in the hope of having to mow less frequently, but doing so can give your lawn a nasty shock and turn it a rather unpleasant brown colour! Aim to mow little and often; once a week from Spring through to Summer is ideal.

Always clear away grass clippings once you've mowed, and twice a year in early Spring and late Autumn, give your lawn a good rake to remove dead grass and moss, known as thatch. Whilst you're at it, aerate the underlying soil by punching holes in the lawn using a fork or fancier aeration tool. This will allow air and water to penetrate the soil and reach down to the grass roots, improving water uptake and leading to a happier lawn.

POND PREDICAMENTS

Ponds are a great way of inviting wildlife into your garden. Toads, newts and frogs will all spawn in water but only if the conditions are right.

One of the most common pond problems is that of green pond syndrome. Green ponds are the result of a build up of algae or blanket weed. These aquatic plants are particularly partial to water with high nutrient levels. The simplest way of avoiding this foul green slime is to reduce the nitrogen levels. Remove any leaves that have fallen in as they will slowly decompose, adding to your nitrogen nightmare. And, as much as they might wish you to, don't overfeed your fish – their food contains high levels of nitrogen which algae will thrive on.

If you decide to pull out any excess weed, always leave it on the side of the pond for a few days so that any unsuspecting wildlife can crawl away.

Hold off on pond maintenance until Autumn – at this point amphibians will have finished breeding but will not yet have gone into hibernation, so you won't run the risk of disturbing them.

... Don't overfeed your fish – their food contains high levels of nitrogen which algae will thrive on.

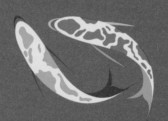

My garden is my most beautiful masterpiece.

Claude Monet

HEDGE YOUR BETS

Unless you want boundaries akin to Sleeping Beauty's forest of thorns, your hedge is going to need a proper bit of pruning every now and again.

Before you reach for the hedge trimmers, check your hedge. Hedges come in a variety of forms: evergreen, deciduous, conifers and box, and they all have their own particular pruning preferences. Trim at the wrong time of year, or too hard, and your hedge will struggle to recover.

The most effective pruning allows sunlight to penetrate growth in the centre of the hedge. Without this sunlight you'll end up with dead, brown branches on the inside.

Hedges have a tendency to become wider at the top, shadowing branches lower down and causing foliage to die back. Aim for a wider bottom and narrower top to allow light to access all parts of the hedge evenly.

Birds love a good hedge, so avoid trimming when they are nesting between the months of April and July.

SUPPORTING SPINDLY STEMS

We all need a bit of support sometimes. Plants are no exception. Start with some stakes, then whack up a wigwam, or try a trellis.

Supports will help prevent your prized plants from getting droopy, and in the worse cases, stems snapping and the whole plant flattening altogether, particularly in wet and windy weather.

You can create your own for free, by bending thick wire or tying together fallen and cut branches to form a framework around the base of your plants. Twiggy sticks work well as a support for peas.

Try to push in supports early on before the plant is on the verge of collapse, rather than waiting until it sits forlornly with a mass of broken stems.

Trees and plants always look like the people they live with, somehow.

Zora Neale Hurston

CREEPY CRAWLY PESTS

Attack of the aphids 93

Ant antics 94

Ghastly grubs 97

The very hungry caterpillar 98

Banishing biting beasts 101

Stingers and suckers 102

On the trail of the slug and snail 105

The slippery soapy spray will stop them getting a foothold and they'll struggle to stay attached to the stems.

ATTACK OF THE APHIDS

These tiny bugs feast on sap and will happily suck your poor plants dry, leaving them wizened and black. Fight back with a three-pronged attack.

While it's not everyone's cup of tea, one of the best ways of removing aphids is to banish all squeamishness and squish them with your fingers. You'll need to keep doing this every few days as aphids reproduce quickly and warm springs and summers can see populations boom.

For those with less destructive tendencies, affected stems can be sprayed with a mixture of washing up liquid diluted in water. Fill a plastic bottle with the solution and then drill a hole in the cap. Squash the bottle to spray the pressured solution directly onto the little suckers. The slippery soapy spray will stop them getting a foothold and they'll struggle to stay attached to the stems.

Like many creepy crawly conundrums, there is generally a heroic insect overlord who preys on gardening pests. This one is no exception. Ladybirds love nothing more than to gorge on aphids. Encourage them into your plot by leaving parts of your garden wild (where they will overwinter). Come Spring, they will emerge and reproduce and both adults and their larvae will obligingly munch their way through large numbers of aphids each day.

ANT ANTICS

Ants are essentially hired thugs who are paid generously to protect their sponsors, the vulnerable aphid.

While the aphids suck the bejesus out of your plants, the ants will zealously defend them, attacking any invading predators with ferocity – including any unfortunate gardener who happens to get in the way. Whilst they won't break the skin, ants can give a painful nip. In payment for their protection, the ants farm the aphids for a bi-product of sap called honey dew.

On their own, ants nests can cause damage to the roots of plants when their nests are in close proximity. As they excavate the soil around the roots, the plant is deprived of water and hey presto, doomed plants.

Before reaching for the ant powder, experiment with some alternative natural solutions. Ants really hate strong odours, so try adding some cayenne pepper or peppermint oil to the affected areas.

Whilst they won't break the skin, ants can give a painful nip.

Everything that slows us down and forces patience, everything that sets us back into the slow circles of nature, is a help. Gardening is an instrument of grace.

May Sarton

GHASTLY GRUBS

They may sound stylish, but leather jackets in a garden are not welcome in any season.

Also known as the larvae of the daddy long legs, these rather unpleasant looking creatures sit in the soil and slurp their way through plant roots (often grass), rather like an Italian eating spaghetti. Chafer grubs and wine weevil larvae share this grubby habit, and this trio of terror will make your beloved lawn and garden plants look very unhappy indeed.

It's easy to pick and squish these stinkers as you come across them, but a more reliable way of defeating them is to use a nematode biological control. Once watered in, the area should be kept nice and moist to allow these wonder worms to do their work.

THE VERY HUNGRY CATERPILLAR

Caterpillars have voracious appetites and can cause havoc when left unchecked on brassicas, munching their way through entire leaves and stripping plants of vegetation.

Although organic, hand picking caterpillars off plants rates pretty low on the enjoyment scale. Bearing in mind that this practice is very time-consuming and isn't always effective, it may be worth investing in a form of biological control such as nematode worms or wasps, which can be ordered directly online.

Although beautiful, butterflies can lay up to 300 eggs at one time, which means A LOT of caterpillars munching their way through your prized plants. Covering plants with fine netting or horticultural fleece can help to prevent butterflies laying eggs in the first place.

Although organic, hand picking caterpillars off plants rates pretty low on the enjoyment scale.

If you're planning to be outside at night, burn some citronella candles to ward off these irksome insects.

BANISHING BITING BEASTS

Biting insects can be a menace in the garden – particularly for those unfortunate individuals that winged whiners find especially appetising.

To help reduce mosquito numbers, start by eradicating any stagnant water, where mosquitoes will congregate and lay their eggs. Empty any buckets and watering cans that have accumulated rainfall and clean any bird baths regularly and replace the water once a week. Mosquitoes don't like running water so if you have a pond, consider installing a simple fountain to deter them.

To avoid unsightly and incredibly itchy red welts, wear long sleeves to cover your arms and trousers to cover your legs. In the summer, when donning long sleeved garb is neither practical nor comfortable, apply a liberal spray of insect repellent.

Avoid being in the garden at dusk, when more biting insects come out. If you're planning to be outside at night, burn some citronella candles to ward off these irksome insects.

Birds such as swallows and bats relish hoovering up small insects like mosquitoes, so encourage them into your garden by installing a bird or bat house.

STINGERS AND SUCKERS

Bees, wasps, mosquitoes and even ants can be a real nuisance in the garden and leave the average gardener leaping around with flailing arms or running for cover. A quick peek in the kitchen cupboards for some home remedies will have you back outside and enjoying your garden in no time.

Bees stings are acidic so can be neutralised with an alkaline solution of bicarbonate of soda (which helpfully also doubles up as a good remedy for an upset stomach). Remove the bee stinger itself by scraping over it with a credit card.

Wasps retain their sting and so can, and will, sting multiple times if they feel threatened. The sting of wasps is alkaline, so neutralise it with a dilute acid such as vinegar or lemon juice.

The pulp of aloe vera is an effective treatment for many skin irritations, including ant and mosquito bites. It is incredibly easy to maintain – keep a pot on your kitchen windowsill for all your insect irritation needs.

Not all weeds are bad! Leave the odd patch of dock – their leaves are excellent at soothing nettle stings.

The pulp of aloe vera is an effective treatment for many skin irritations.

One of the worst mistakes you can make as a gardener is to think you're in charge.

Janet Gillespie

ON THE TRAIL OF THE SLUG AND SNAIL

Leaving a silvery trail of slime in their wake, slugs and snails wreak havoc in the garden, their rasping mouths creating untold destruction as they munch their way through prized plants and vegetables.

Particularly partial to seedlings and shoots, critters are most active after dark or during wet weather. Traditional deterrents include barriers, such as a layer of eggshells, coffee grounds or mulch around plants, or traps, such as jam jars filled with salt water.

As tempting as it may be to throw the meddlesome molluscs over the fence, it's worth bearing in mind that, much like grumbling neighbours, they do have a tendency to return.

ANIMAL PESTS

Overcoming pigeon pests 108

Managing moggy misadventures 111

Cracking canine calamities 112

Reducing rabbit ruination 115

Making nice with mice 116

Minimising mole mishaps 119

Fighting foxy fiends 120

Deer, oh dear 123

Squirrel sorrows 124

OVERCOMING PIGEON PESTS

Generally, inviting birds into the garden has a positive effect on the environment – they hoover up pests and the sound of their sweet song sets a relaxing tone for an hour or two of weeding. But some feathered friends can also be foes.

Pigeons and wood pigeons go a bit bananas for brassicas and have a propensity for peas. They will strip the entire plant of foliage – often only leaving the stalks.

They also make the most monumental mess. If pigeons have decided that your garden offers a good opportunity for a feed and have taken up residence you'll know about it. Garden furniture, children's swings and slides will all get the pigeon poo treatment.

Cover up crops with wide netting, secured with pegs, or grow them in a fruit cage to prevent the pigeons from reaching the plants. Bird scarers may look and sound like a good idea but generally aren't effective against bird bombardment.

Pigeons and wood pigeons go a bit bananas for brassicas and have a propensity for peas.

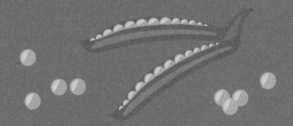

Cats love nothing more than a well dug patch of soil to do their 'business'.

MANAGING MOGGY MISADVENTURES

The fluffy and friendly domestic cat is no doubt a popular pet, but can make a massive mess of recently dug and planted areas.

Cats love nothing more than a well dug patch of soil to do their 'business'. To remove this temptation, cover up recently dug beds with mulch, or lay pruned branches or stems across the soil at angles, or pointing upwards. Chicken wire or netting pinned across the soil surface will also help to deter unwanted digging and deposits.

Moggies have highly sensitive noses and can also be effectively deterred using citrus odours. Try dropping orange peelings over the worst affected areas, or use a shop-bought repellent specifically formulated for this purpose. Other strong scents, such as crushed black pepper, are also worth a try.

As a last resort, consider a commercial electronic cat scarer that will emit a high pitched sound (which cannot be heard by humans) when any movement is detected.

CRACKING CANINE CALAMITIES

Man's best friend is not always a friend of the garden. Dogs like to dig. A lot. Especially when left to their own devices. Equally at home digging in flowerbeds and lawns, turn your back and before you can whistle for walkies, your newly planted shrub is upended.

Even small fences around your borders will help to prevent your dog from entering and causing canine carnage. Consider creating a designated and sacrificial digging area if your pooch can't help themselves.

Their innate sense of curiosity means that dogs do have a habit of escaping gardens if they are not sealed securely. Make sure all boundaries are securely fastened to ground level and cannot be easily dug underneath. Check them regularly to make sure no holes have started to appear.

Dogs also love a good chew and they tend not to discriminate. Gardening shoes, hoses and decking are all up for grabs. Keep what you can out of reach and try providing some garden toys to keep them entertained and distracted.

Their innate sense of curiosity means that dogs do have a habit of escaping gardens.

A lush, established garden can be demolished over the course of a single night.

REDUCING RABBIT RUINATION

Rabbits ruining your veg patch? Need to take action? Make like Mr McGregor and hop to it.

Rabbits build their warrens in areas of dense shrub cover so if your garden backs onto woodland, chances are you'll be familiar with them. They may look cuddly and innocent, but they eat pretty much anything that has succulent shoots and leaves. Once rabbits take hold (they really do breed like rabbits), a lush, established garden can be demolished over the course of a single night.

Rabbits tend to be most active between dusk and dawn, so you're unlikely to see them in the day, but 'bunny bumbles' (droppings) are pretty easy to identify and will give you an obvious clue as to what you're dealing with.

If you're keen to get rid of these bunny hopping bandits, install a wire barrier around the perimeter of your garden, sinking the wire below the soil surface so they can't dig under it. Or if you simply want to protect that single giant carrot, just wire directly around that.

MAKING NICE WITH MICE

Mice are real mischief makers – they aren't fussy and enjoy a varied diet of newly planted bulbs, seedlings and even the bark of trees if food is scarce.

Mice are particularly partial to the seeds of beans, peas and sweetcorn; rows originally planted with meticulous precision can end up looking a little sparse once seedlings emerge. When temperatures dip in winter, mice will seek refuge in sheds and greenhouses where their tiny tooth marks cause damage to stored fruit and veg, and germinating seeds.

Mice are more of an annoyance than a severe pest and so unless you see a population boom, it's best to leave them be and manage the damage they cause. To reduce nocturnal nibblings, start off seeds indoors, rather than in the greenhouse, where the rodents can't reach them. Place wire netting over bulbs after you've planted them and then cover with compost. The shoots will still make it through but the mice will be disappointed.

To reduce nocturnal nibblings, start off seeds indoors, rather than in the greenhouse.

Moles do have their benefits – the topsoil they discard is a perfect base for potting compost.

MINIMISING MOLE MISHAPS

What moles lack in eyesight they more than make up for in digging prowess.

With long front paws perfect for shovelling earth, and silky soft dark fur, these lords of the earth spend most, if not all, of their lives underground, happily searching for earthworms (their favourite snack). As they form their labyrinthine tunnels, the excavated soil is pushed to the surface, creating molehills. This is the first and only clue that moles have moved in, and pretty much a complete nightmare for any lawn aficionados.

Interestingly, moles don't like noise, and some gardeners have reported successful attempts moving them on by of playing a bit of drum and bass down the mole tunnel. They are also incredibly sensitive to smell, so pick something that smells bad (really smelly cheese rinds or hay soaked in sour milk or yoghurt) and pop it in the mole hole. They will hopefully get the message and decamp to another territory.

FIGHTING FOXY FIENDS

Apart from their nocturnal banshee screaming (a sure wake up call for even the deepest of sleepers), trademark signs of foxes can include trampling of plants, digging, distribution of unrecognisable food debris and, perhaps most undesirably, droppings. Foxes also love a good chew toy and aren't fussy about the form they take: hose pipes, children's toys and shoes are all perfectly acceptable items for jaw exercises.

Foxes are incredibly difficult to get rid of and so managing their destructive habits and gently discouraging them to leave are your best defence. Try to find a way of living as harmoniously as possible together.

Don't bother installing expensive fences in a bid to prevent access – they will leap over with the grace of an Olympic gymnast, or dig and crawl underneath.

Top tips for reducing fox damage:

- Fill in any holes dug by foxes straightaway. If left, you may come back to find a fully formed den.

- Do not use bonemeal or other animal derived fertilisers as the smell is quite intoxicating for these furry fiends.

- Use plants that can withstand the excited trampling of your nightly visitors.

- Always clear up after any meals outside – food left out at night is an open invitation for foxy visitors.

If you're happy with the odd sneaky nibble, provide feeding alternatives by keeping part of your garden wild.

DEER, OH DEAR

With their bambi-like eyes and graceful gait, gardeners can be easily seduced by the beauty of deer. That is until their naughty nibbling habits become a very noticeable nightmare.

Fallow, roe and muntjac deer can all make their presence felt in the garden. They'll nibble the tips off young shoots, and males of the species will rub their antlers against trees, leaving the bark in a frayed and forlorn mess.

Unlike rabbits, who make a clean cut with their incisors, deer leave ragged munch marks on plants and, unless you've already caught them in the act, this will be a key clue to what you're dealing with.

The only failsafe way to protect your garden against these doe-eyed destroyers is to install a fence that they can't scramble under or jump over. Plastic tubing will also help to protect trees against the worst of deery head butts.

If you're happy with the odd sneaky nibble, provide feeding alternatives by keeping part of your garden wild. As far as deer are concerned, brambles, dandelions and even knotweed are all perfectly suitable fodder options for a five star culinary experience.

SQUIRREL SORROWS

The acrobatic exhibitionists of the garden, grey squirrels, offer no end of entertainment with their death-defying leaps and dives, flying with finesse from branch to branch. Unhappily, their continually growing front teeth means they are constantly gnawing to keep these incisors in check!

Squirrel destruction isn't terribly selective. They will strip bark from trees, dig up seeds and bulbs and eat fruits and vegetables. To the frustration of many a wildlife-friendly gardener, squirrels are exceptionally skilled at emptying bird feeders, and if that weren't bad enough, they will even raid the birds' nests, stealing and eating the eggs.

Squirrels may not look like deviant criminals, but they are incredibly intelligent and notoriously difficult to control. Dogs make great squirrel deterrents, but there are two alternative ways to deter them: through distraction or the use of physical barriers.

It may sound counterproductive, but providing a decoy food stash specifically for squirrels can distract them from other, less readily available, food sources (i.e. your garden plants and produce).

If you opt for a physical barrier, don't bother with anything plastic – the squirrels will gnaw their way through with ease. For foolproof protection, wire netting is the only way to go. Surround trees and plants with wire mesh and place it on top of newly planted bulbs.

To the frustration of many a wildlife-friendly gardener, squirrels are exceptionally skilled at emptying bird feeders.

NOTES

Gardening is a metaphor for life, teaching you to nourish new life and weed out that which cannot succeed.

Nelson Mandela

NOTES

When the world wearies and society fails to satisfy,
there is always the garden.

Minnie Aumonier

NOTES

_____

_____

_____

_____

_____

_____

_____

_____

_____

_____

_____

_____

_____

_____

A garden is a grand teacher. It teaches patience and careful watchfulness; it teaches industry and thrift; above all it teaches entire trust.

Gertrude Jekyll